SHARE MY MEDITATIONS

Living Devotions
for
Personal and Group Use

SHARE MY MEDITATIONS

Living Devotions
for
Personal and Group Use

by

Catrina Parrott Whaley

BAKER BOOK HOUSE
Grand Rapids, Michigan

PHOTOLITHOPRINTED BY CUSHING - MALLOY, INC.
ANN ARBOR, MICHIGAN, UNITED STATES OF AMERICA
1 9 6 7

CONTENTS

Be Prepared

We are often neglectful of our spiritual natures and are therefore caught off-guard by sudden, unexpected, trying situations. Indiscreet words and hasty actions plague us. A Christian is likened to a soldier on duty dressed in the whole armor of God, ready for whatever comes. He prepares his mind through meditation and communion with God and is therefore aware of him and conscious of his responsibility to represent him. Spiritual sensitivity and response to his love are thus strengthened through this association and he can act with deliberation instead of haste.

★　★　★

Watch and pray that you may not enter into temptation; the spirit indeed is willing, but the flesh is weak. — *Matt. 26:41*

Be not rash with your mouth, nor let your heart be hasty to utter a word before God, for God is in heaven, and you upon earth; therefore let your words be few. — *Eccles. 5:2*

If any one purifies himself from what is ignoble, then he will be a vessel for noble use, consecrated and useful to the master of the house, ready for any good work. So shun youthful passions and aim at righteousness, faith, love, and peace, along with those who call upon the Lord from a pure heart. — *2 Tim. 2:21-22*

★　★　★

Ready to go, ready to bear,
Ready to watch and pray;
Ready to stand aside and give,
Till he shall clear the way.

Ready to speak, ready to think,
Ready with heart and brain;
Ready to stand where he sees fit,
Ready to stand the strain.

— Anonymous

Our Father, may we be prepared to stand the strains of daily contacts in the market place, in the school and in the home. We thank thee for thy protecting care. May we be ready to speak from experiences, with conviction and with wisdom about thee if we are questioned. May our words be backed by quality deeds. May we be careful of our speech, but ready to speak when necessary. Amen.

Live Your Faith

God never promised an easy life, but Christians can give form and substance to their faith by living it in a harsh world. They belong to that fellowship, the church, that strengthens them in the service of God and helps overcome the feeling of isolation. Their way of living does not evade or avoid peril or troubles but gives them strength to meet these things courageously. Christians are the hope of the world in the place where they are. Pastors could ask many of their long-time absentee members, "Where have you been?" The church cannot do its work without the presence, support, and prayers of each member.

★　★　★

I have said this to you, that in me you may have peace. In the world you have tribulation; but be of good cheer, I have overcome the world. — *John 16:33*

In him was life, and the life was the light of men. The light shines in the darkness, and the darkness has not overcome it. There was a man sent from God, whose name was John. He came for testimony, to bear witness to the light, that all might believe through him. He was not the light, but came to bear witness to the light. — *John 1:4-8*

But I say to you, Love your enemies and pray for those who persecute you, so that you may be sons of your Father who is in heaven; for he makes his sun rise on the evil and on the good, and sends rain on the just and on the unjust. — *Matt. 5:44-45*

★　★　★

We bless thee, Lord, for all this common life
Can give of rest and joy amidst its strife;
For earth and trees and seas and clouds and springs;
For work, and all the lessons that it brings.

For each achievement human toil can reach;
For all the patriots win, and poets teach;
For the old light that gleams in history's page,
For the new hope that shines on each new age.

— Frederick M. White, 1873

★   ★   ★

O kind and holy Father, we thank thee for providing all the necessary things of life along with many "extras." May we meet the demand of all our love and strength by giving freely in thy service. May we be steadfast and unchanging in our devotion to thee as we live day by day on the earth. May we be found faithful in the work of thy church. Amen.

Follow Christ

Jesus, always kind to outcasts, went home with Zacchaeus, the commissioner of taxes at Jericho. It was a known fact that his wealth had been acquired by defrauding the people. Jesus' visit started Zacchaeus on a new track. He began to repay those he had wronged. Fortunately, he could make restoration. His actions declared that he loved God and therefore loved his fellowman. The spirit of love or hate cannot be hidden from those toward whom it is directed. His center of life shifted from self to God. This is the best insurance and assurance for each of us in life.

★　★　★

And he called to him the multitude with his disciples and said to them, "If any man would come after me, let him deny himself and take up his cross and follow me. For whoever would save his life will lose it; and whoever loses his life for my sake and the gospel's will save it. For what does it profit a man, to gain the whole world and forefeit his life? — *Mark 8:34-35*

And Zacchaeus stood and said to the Lord, "Behold, Lord, the half of my goods I give to the poor; and if I have defrauded any one of anything, I restore it fourfold." — *Luke 19:8*

★　★　★

I heard the voice of Jesus say,
"Behold, I freely give
The living water; thirsty one,
Stoop down, and drink, and live."
I came to Jesus and I drank
Of that life-giving stream:
My thirst was quenched, my soul revived,
And now I live in him.

— Horatius Bonar, 1808-1889

11

O God, we praise and adore thee. Be with those who suffer innocently because of avarice and blunders of others. We are grateful for thy redeeming grace. May we all have the courage to let thee "come alive" in us. May we right the wrongs that can be corrected, but willingly leave the others in thy hands. Make us willing to accept thy gift of forgiveness for ourselves and others. Amen.

Talking

Talking, like many things, can be good or bad. Fire in the furnace heats the house, but fire unconfined and raging destroys the house. Kind words spread joy and happiness. Malignant words can produce psychological hurts and destroy man's most infinite, yet earthly, possession, that is, his influence for good. Sowing deadly doubt and suspicion has resulted in tragedy. We must choose our words for ourselves. We each speak our own piece. May we make choices that will both bless us and make us a blessing. To refrain from speaking ill will bring gratification and peace to a man and his friends.

★   ★   ★

O Lord, who shall sojourn in thy tent?
    Who shall dwell on thy holy hill?
He who walks blamelessly, and does what is right,
    and speaks truth from his heart;
who does not slander with his tongue,
    and does no evil to his friend,
    nor takes up a reproach against his neighbor; . . .
who swears to his own hurt and does not change.
                                            —*Ps. 15:1-4*

★   ★   ★

Dear Lord and Father of mankind,
Forgive our foolish ways;
Reclothe us in our rightful mind;
In purer lives thy service find,
In deeper rev'rence, praise.

Drop thy still dews of quietness,
Till all our strivings cease;
Take from our souls the strain and stress,
And let our ordered lives confess
The beauty of thy peace.
— John G. Whittier, 1807-1892

★　　★　　★

Our God and Father, we thank thee for thy presence in our inmost sanctuary. Under the powerful influence of thy love may we forgive those who have wronged us even as we seek thy forgiveness for our own hasty, angry judgments. May we not live contrary to Christian kindness this day. Amen.

Love Is Kind

A critical mind makes one tense and unhappy. To be constantly speaking of the undesirable traits of people builds up walls that are insurmountable. To lessen tension, see the best and be complimentary of work well done. We all need appreciation and encouragement. Increasing a person's self-esteem will create happiness in which you will share. We cannot climb up by lowering another person. Love is kind. It is not always finding fault, but covers a multitude of them. Love is courteous. It does not glorify itself. May we all pray for hearts filled with God's love. May it spill over on our fellow-man.

★　★　★

Love is patient and kind; love is not jealous or boastful; it is not arrogant or rude. Love does not insist on its own way; it is not irritable or resentful; it does not rejoice at wrong, but rejoices in the right. Love bears all things, believes all things, hopes all things, endures all things.

Love never ends; as for prophecies, they will pass away; as for tongues, they will cease; as for knowledge, it will pass away. For our knowledge is imperfect and our prophecy is imperfect; but when the perfect comes, the imperfect will pass away.

1 Cor. 13:4-10

★　★　★

Give of your best to the Master,
Give of the strength of your youth;
Throw your soul's fresh glowing ardor
Into the battle for truth:
Jesus has set the example,
Dauntless was he, young and brave;
Give him your loyal devotion,
Give him the best that you have.
　　　　—Howard B. Grose, 1851-1939

Our Father, may we be relaxed, happy, appreciative persons. Make us more thoughtful and kind in dealing with others. May our love be Christ-like enough to cover the defects of others. Take away our critical attitudes and give us patience. Forgive us for being rude and resentful and give us strength to bear all things without complaining. Amen.

Things

In our civilization the carnal mind is dominant because material achievements have surpassed the moral and spiritual ones. Things order our lives and consume our time and energy to such an extent that they almost possess us. We need to ask ourselves, Do we have these things, or do they have us? We have sacrificed our inner peace to obtain them and to keep them. Our bodies are the temples of God. We have ready access to his inexhaustible spiritual resources. When we let people and things hurt us, it is natural to strike back, but this is not good. It hurts others and creates more tension. We need to draw on God's available strength.

For those who live according to the flesh set their minds on the things of the flesh, but those who live according to the Spirit set their minds on the things of the Spirit. To set the mind on the flesh is death, but to set the mind on the Spirit is life and peace. For the mind that is set on the flesh is hostile to God; it does not submit to God's law, indeed it cannot; and those who are in the flesh cannot please God.

But you are not in the flesh, you are in the Spirit, if the Spirit of God really dwells in you. Any one who does not have the Spirit of Christ does not belong to him. — *Rom. 8:5-9*

I am resolved no longer to linger,
Charmed by the world's delight;
Things that are higher, things that are nobler,
These have allured my sight.

I am resolved to follow the Savior,
Faithful and true each day;
Heed what he sayeth, do what he willeth,
He is the living way.

— Palmer Hartsough, 1844-1932

O Holy Father, we thank thee for the night's rest and the day with its new opportunities to serve thee and to extend thy kingdom of love. May we have the inner serenity and peace that come from living nobly and well in difficult situations. May thy power be manifested today in thy people as their lives "speak" of thee to others. May we be strong enough not to strike back at those who provoke us today. May we not even allow ourselves to be provoked. Amen.

Faith's Foundation

Our very existence is linked with God. Man is always seeking God — the one true God or something he elevates to first place in his life. Anything that makes him unaware of God and to which he has surrendered his well-being may become an idol, a god. Success is an example. Many modern men are totally involved with it. They expend all of their time, thought, and energy on achieving it. They sacrifice their health, the companionship of their family, and sometimes life itself for it. In a total surrender to God, there can be no reservations. Faith claims the whole personality — otherwise man fails in his fulfillment. We are certain of faith's foundation — Jesus Christ — who is manifest as crucified.

For "In him we live and move and have our being."
— *Acts 17:28a*

And without faith it is impossible to please him. For whoever would draw near to God must believe that he exists and that he rewards those who seek him. — *Heb. 11:6*

Therefore, since we are justified by faith, we have peace with God through our Lord Jesus Christ. Through him we have obtained access to this grace in which we stand, and we rejoice in our hope of sharing the glory of God. — *Rom. 5:1-2*

Remember your leaders . . . imitate their faith. Jesus Christ is the same yesterday and today and for ever. — *Heb. 13:7-8*

> *What is faith's foundation strong?*
> *What awakes my lips to song?*
> *He who bore my sinful load,*
> *Purchased for me peace with God,*
> *Jesus Christ, the crucified.*

This is that great thing I know;
This delights and stirs me so;
Faith in him who died to save,
Him who triumphed o'er the grave,
Jesus Christ, the crucified.
— Johann C. Schwedler, 1672-1730
Tr. by B. H. Kennedy, 1804-1889

★   ★   ★

O God, we thank thee for Christ, the crucified yet living Lord. We earnestly desire to love thee with our very existence, our whole being — hearts, souls, minds, and bodies. We thank thee for those who have lived by faith and have been triumphant in life and death. Amen.

Stepping Stones

It is a mistake to say harmful things about anyone. To refrain strengthens character and adds to peace of mind. Many people condemn themselves and worry too much about their errors. Evaluate them and drop them. Forgive yourself. Forgive others, too. God forgives you. Gladstone said, "No man ever became great or good except through many and great mistakes." Human beings are imperfect. Forget about saving face. Learning how not to do a thing can be a stepping stone instead of a stumbling block if we so choose. Try again. Many people have acknowledged that their mistakes led to their success.

Do your best to present yourself to God as one approved, a workman who has no need to be ashamed, rightly handling the word of truth. Avoid such godless chatter, for it will lead people into more and more ungodliness, and their talk will eat its way like gangrene. — *2 Tim. 2:15-17*

If any one thinks he is religious, and does not bridle his tongue but deceives his heart, this man's religion is vain. Religion that is pure and undefiled before God and the Father is this: to visit orphans and widows in their affliction, and to keep oneself unstained from the world. — *James 1:26-27*

Lord, as we thy name profess,
May our hearts thy love confess;
And in all our praise of thee,
May our lips and lives agree.

21

May thy yoke be meekly worn,
May thy cross be bravely borne,
Make us patient, gentle, kind,
Pure in life and heart and mind.
— E. P. Parker, 1880

★   ★   ★

Our Father, may we develop self-control in all the areas of our lives. Help us to be especially careful of our thoughts that they may be centered on true, just, and honorable things. May we have the mastery over our minds. Help us to be moderate in all things and to be careful in all things. We thank thee for thy love so deep, so broad, so high and so unfailing. Amen.

The Good Life

So much evil in the world has made man anxious about the good life. Our Christianity is established around the crucified and risen Christ. To give life to others, he faced death. We must come to grips with him and reach for him in our own stumbling, falling way. Faith is a matter of personal concern. Loving God with all our being is the demand of faith. Christ is all we need to know; he is the way, the truth, the life. He meets us now if we come to him in sincerity. The Bible will speak to your heart as you read it. It will guide you.

★　★　★

But in every nation any one who fears him and does what is right is acceptable to him. You know the word which he sent to Israel, preaching good news of peace by Jesus Christ (he is Lord of all), the word which was proclaimed throughout all Judea, beginning from Galilee after the baptism which John preached: how God anointed Jesus of Nazareth with the Holy Spirit and with power; how he went about doing good and healing all that were oppressed by the devil, for God was with him. And we are witnesses to all that he did both in the country of the Jews and in Jerusalem. They put him to death by hanging him on a tree.

— *Acts 10:35-39*

★　★　★

Cast thy burden on the Lord,
Lean thou only on his Word;
Ever will he be thy stay,
Tho' the heav'ns shall melt away.

He will gird thee by his pow'r
In the weary, fainting hour;
Lean thou strong upon his Word,
Cast thy burden on the Lord.

— George Rawson, 1857
(1807-1889)

★ ★ ★

O God, our protector, and our guide, be with us in our daily living. Give us compassion one for the other and make us courteous in all our dealings. Refrain our tongues from speaking evil and help us to follow only the good. Cause us to love thee more each day and to live a life worthy of thy everlasting love. Clear away the ugliness of envy and selfishness, we pray. Amen.

Serving

Do you stand for right? When disagreements arise, check your motives. Some people feel that their will must predominate. With wisdom and a sound heart, a genuine person can step aside and let someone take the place that was rightfully his. Learning to adjust, to give in, demonstrates a great spirit. Take a modest responsibility and magnify it by an unusual performance. This glorifies God. Do not seek a place of esteem in the church but rather a place of service. Earn the honor of a job faithfully done.

★　★　★

I would rather be a door keeper in the house of my God
   than dwell in the tents of wickedness.
For the Lord God is a sun and shield;
   he bestows favor and honor.
No good thing does the Lord withhold
   from those who walk uprightly.
O Lord of hosts,
   blessed is the man who trusts in thee!

— Ps. 84:10b-12

But then what return did you get from the things of which you are now ashamed? The end of those things is death. But now that you have been set free from sin and have become slaves of God, the return you get is sanctification and its end, eternal life.

— Rom. 6:21-22

Must Jesus bear the cross alone,
And all the world go free?
No, there's a cross for ev'ry one,
And there's a cross for me.

The consecrated cross I'll bear
Till death shall set me free;
And then go home my crown to wear,
For there's a crown for me.
— Thomas Shepherd, 1665-1739

★   ★   ★

Our Father, we praise thee for thy goodness and power and especially for thy saving grace. Save us from the pride of selfish desires. May we give of our best to whatever task we perform. Give us the spirit of humility that can serve well in lesser places. May we remember that Jesus took a towel and girded himself and washed the disciples' feet. We thank thee for his example. Amen.

Higher Goals

All people should exercise and eat properly in order to be physically fit. Good health enables us to develop mentally and spiritually. Those who hunger and thirst for righteousness shall be filled. Only a relationship with Christ that brings forth spiritual fruit is real. "Nominal" Christianity does not add joy, peace or virtue to life. By giving preference to the higher things, we work and attain them. We deny ourselves to help others. What is happening today in your life? What are your hopes? What are my hopes?

★   ★   ★

Every athlete exercises self-control in all things. They do it to receive a perishable wreath, but we an imperishable. Well, I do not run aimlessly, I do not box as one beating the air; but I pommel my body and subdue it, lest after preaching to others I myself should be disqualified. — *1 Cor. 9:25-27*

Do not be conformed to this world but be transformed by the renewal of your mind, that you may prove what is the will of God, what is good and acceptable and perfect. — *Rom. 12:2*

Fight the good fight of the faith; take hold of the eternal life to which you were called when you made the good confession in the presence of many witnesses. — *1 Tim. 6:12*

★   ★   ★

My soul, be on thy guard;
Ten thousand foes arise;
The hosts of sin are pressing hard
To draw thee from the skies.

O watch and fight and pray;
The battle ne'er give o'er;
Renew it boldly every day,
And help divine implore.

— George Heath, 1750-1822

★　　★　　★

Our heavenly Father, we thank thee for thy mercy and grace. We thank thee for the spiritual unrest of our beings that draws us to thee. We thank thee for the courage to face danger, for strength to perform our tasks and for the joys of life. May we be truly Christian men and women in our living this day. Amen.

Christian Vocations

The fact that life is not divided into secular and sacred could be a revolutionary idea if really believed because it makes every vocation a religious one. The Christian witness is to "come alive" within it. It is the place of involvement where we can participate actively in our mission of being the light of the world, the salt of the earth. We can do this by giving an honest day's work and by an attitude of helpfulness. A job well done is a Christian witness. All believers, whatever their occupation, are in a full-time Christian vocation.

★   ★   ★

. . . Lead a life worthy of the calling to which you have been called, with all lowliness and meekness, with patience, forbearing one another in love, eager to maintain the unity of the Spirit in the bond of peace. There is one body and one Spirit, just as you were called to the one hope that belongs to your call, one Lord, one faith, one baptism, one God and Father of us all, who is above all and through all and in all. But grace was given to each of us according to the measure of Christ's gift. Therefore it is said,

"When he ascended on high he led a host of captives,
and he gave gifts to men."
— *Eph. 4:1b-8*

★   ★   ★

Onward, Christian soldiers,
Marching as to war,
With the cross of Jesus,
Going on before.
Christ the royal Master,
Leads against the foe;
Forward into battle,
See, his banners go.
— S. Baring Gould, 1865

29

Holy Father, as we go about the business of making a living, grant the realization that thou canst be glorified by our doing our best in the humblest or the highest profession. May we develop by rendering good service and thus be prepared to do even greater work. Keep us happy and faithful in the thought that we are contributing to the world's good when we fill our place well. Amen.

Our Religious Life

The church is not a building. It is the gathering of those people who belong to a particular group of believers. Their influence should be felt in the business and political affairs of the community. They are Christ's representatives there. To many people, life seems to be largely secular, but to Christians life is all holy. Those who become totally involved with Christ have a transforming effect by their manner of living and sharing with others. Unless they show a burning zeal and devotion to their faith, they fail and remain undisturbing and ineffective in their witness.

★ ★ ★

So Paul, standing in the middle of the Areopagus, said: "Men of Athens, I perceive that in every way you are very religious. For as I passed along, and observed the objects of your worship, I found also an altar with this inscription, 'To an unknown god.' What therefore you worship as unknown, this I proclaim to you. The God who made the world and everything in it, being Lord of heaven and earth, does not live in shrines made by man, nor is he served by human hands, as though he needed anything, since he himself gives to all men life and breath and everything."

— *Acts 17:22-25*

★ ★ ★

Laborers of Christ, arise,
And gird you for the toil,
The dew of promise from the skies
Already cheers the soil.

Go where the sick recline,
Where mourning hearts deplore;
And where the sons of sorrow pine,
Dispense your hallowed love.

— L. H. Sigourney

Our Father in heaven, how gracious, loving and kind thou art. May we demonstrate our love by effective Christian living growing out of our constant communion with thee. We are grateful to thee for letting us be thy co-laborers in the world, especially when we think of thee as the giver of life, breath and everything. Help thy church to have a disturbing influence in our own lives and in the broader life of the community. Amen.

Ministers of Life

Every church member is an assistant to the pastor because he has the same command to be a witness. He is a co-worker in communicating his Christian beliefs and convictions. His witness is made valid by his words and actions bearing the same testimony. The temptation to talk rather than act is great. A believer's vocation is a Christian one for the very reason that he is a Christian engaged in it. The way he conducts his business is of spiritual import. This cannot be avoided. He is either faithful or unfaithful in helping to make Christ known among the people.

We always thank God, the Father of our Lord Jesus Christ, when we pray for you, because we have heard of your faith in Christ Jesus and of the love which you have for all the saints, because of the hope laid up for you in heaven. Of this you have heard before in the word of truth, the gospel which has come to you, as indeed in the whole world it is bearing fruit and growing — so among yourselves, from the day you heard and understood the grace of God in truth. — *Col. 1:3-6*

★   ★   ★

Let there be light, Lord God of hosts,
Let there be wisdom on the earth!
Let broad humanity have birth;
Let there be deeds, instead of boasts.

Within our passioned hearts instil
The calm that endeth strain and strife;
Make us thy ministers of life;
Purge us from lusts that curse and kill.
> — William M. Vories, 1880-
> American Peace Society

Our heavenly Father, we praise thee for thy salvation so freely given and for thy mercy and goodness bestowed daily upon us. May we serve thee gladly and proclaim thy love. May our words and actions bear the same testimony. May we do our best because we love thee. May our thoughts be the highest and purest. Also, O God, do not let us be a hindrance because of complacency and indifference. Be with the perplexed and depressed, the weary and sick; suit thy blessing to their needs, we pray. Amen.

Finding the Good

There are people who bring out the best in us because they love us and let it be known. We can all become skilled in this art. Finding the good in people is a delightful way to help. Encouragement makes life run more smoothly. It indicates patience, friendliness and helpfulness. Praise is an excellent cure for strained relations. Love people for their virtues. Love them if they have no outstanding ones. God loved us while we were yet sinners. He suffered in the giving of his Son and Jesus suffered in the giving of his life because he loved us so much. We are sometimes called upon to prove our love by the manner in which we suffer misunderstandings and misjudgments.

★　★　★

For God so loved the world that he gave his only Son, that whoever believes in him should not perish but have eternal life. For God sent the Son into the world, not to condemn the world, but that the world might be saved through him. He who believes in him is not condemned; he who does not believe is condemned already, because he has not believed in the name of the only Son of God. And this is the judgment, that the light has come into the world, and men loved darkness rather than light, because their deeds were evil. — *John* 3:16-19

The Father loves the Son, and has given all things into his hand. He who believes in the Son has eternal life; he who does not obey the Son shall not see life, but the wrath of God rests upon him. *John 3:35-36*

★　★　★

Love divine, all loves excelling,
Joy of heaven, to earth come down;
Fix in us thy humble dwelling;
All thy faithful mercies crown.

Jesus, thou art all compassion,
Pure, unbounded love thou art;
Visit us with thy salvation;
Enter every trembling heart.

— Charles Wesley, 1747
(1707-1788)

★　　★　　★

O God, our Father, our minds cannot fathom thy wonderful love. We praise thee for it and ask thee to make our spirits loving, too. Our God, we realize the great need of thy love in every human heart expressing itself in our relations one with another. May we impart some fragrance to the lives of others. Amen.

The Greatest Power

Jesus gave a new meaning and a new influence to life through prayer. He has trusted us with this great power and has told us to use it without ceasing. . . . When we feel independent and self-sufficient, we tend to forget God. But when we recognize him as the source of all our blessings, we continue to bless him and to depend on him. When we surrender to him, he changes us from selfish beings and uses us in carrying out his will. He has not given us the ability to change his will by our prayers, but he has made it possible for us to be changed. Prayer releases wisdom and understanding to those who are prepared to use them.

★　★　★

Rejoice always, pray constantly, give thanks in all circumstances; for this is the will of God in Christ Jesus for you. Do not quench the Spirit, do not despise prophesying, but test everything; hold fast what is good, abstain from every form of evil.

May the God of peace himself sanctify you wholly; and may your spirit and soul and body be kept sound and blameless at the coming of our Lord Jesus Christ. He who calls you is faithful, and he will do it.

Brethren, pray for us. — *1 Thess. 5:16-25*

★　★　★

O God, we pray for all mankind,
The nations far astray;
We plead that all thy grace may find,
In this thy gracious day.

Thou knowest, Lord, man's sinful state,
The source of human woe,
His evil heart, his greed and hate,
But whither can he go?

Help all the nations, near and far,
Awake, thy glory see;
Behold the Bright and Morning Star,
The Christ of Calvary!
— Howard J. Conover, 1850-1922

★　★　★

Lord God, our Father, all the power in the universe is thine and we are thine. Help us to totally surrender ourselves to thee so that thy power may be available through us to the furtherance of thy work. We confess that we have failed to live up to our own standards and deplore how far short we have been from thine. We seek thy help. Amen.

A Peaceful Church

In our democratic age with people seeking material riches and modern advantages, conflicts arise within the church as well as without. Religious feelings are intense, but Christians are to make every effort to live at peace with all people, especially their brethren. Agree to disagree agreeably. It is unreasonable to withhold your good will from people. Do everything possible, even to giving up your way, to develop a peaceful atmosphere. Patience and kindness help to keep the church unity and create harmony and good will. It is often best to stand back and let the crowd go on.

★ ★ ★

Guard your steps when you go to the house of God; to draw near to listen is better than to offer the sacrifice of fools; for they do not know that they are doing evil. Be not rash with your mouth . . . let your words be few. —*Eccles 5:12*

And the Lord's servant must not be quarrelsome but kindly to every one, an apt teacher, forbearing correcting his opponents with gentleness. God may perhaps grant that they will repent and come to know the truth, and they may escape from the snare of the devil, after being captured by him to do his will.

But understand this, that in the last days there will come times of stress. — *2 Tim. 2:24-26; 3:1*

★ ★ ★

Spirit of grace, oh, deign to dwell
Within thy church below!
Make her in holiness excel,
With purer devotion glow.

Let peace within her walls be found;
Let all her sons unite,
To spread with grateful zeal around
Her clear and shining light.

— Harriet Auber, 1773-1862

★　★　★

Our Father, may we really be ready to render lowly service, "ready to suffer grief or pain, ready to stand the test." Be with those who are frustrated in their life plans. Help them to be contented in doing other things worthily. May they develop patience and understanding for others. O God, keep our ambitions from outreaching our abilities. Give us the will to live at peace with others. Amen.

Inward Reality

If God is not real in our mind and thoughts and first in our affections, we cannot hallow his name. We deny him by anxiety, by inconsistent behavior and hypocrisy. Sunday has long been the set-aside day for man to give extra attention to his soul, for man to observe as a time of shared worship, for man to be keenly aware of the inward reality of God's presence with him. We disregard this opportunity for spiritual renewal at our own risk. In a congregation of like-minded people there is inspiration and strength to be gained.

★ ★ ★

And the Pharisees and the scribes asked him, "Why do your disciples not live according to the tradition of the elders, but eat with hands defiled?" And he said to them, "Well did Isaiah prophesy of you hypocrites, as it is written,

> but their heart is far from me;
> 'This people honor me with their lips,
> in vain do they worship me,
> teaching as doctrines the precepts of men.'

You leave the commandment of God, and hold fast the tradition of men." — *Mark 7:5-8*

"But the hour is coming, and now is, when the true worshipers will worship the Father in spirit and truth, for such the Father seeks to worship him." — *John 4:23*

★ ★ ★

> *This is the day the Lord hath made;*
> *He calls the hours his own;*
> *Let heaven rejoice, let earth be glad,*
> *And praise surround the throne.*

41

Blest be the Lord, who comes to men
With messages of grace;
Who comes, in God his Father's name,
To save our sinful race.

— Isaac Watts, 1674-1748

★ ★ ★

O Lord our help at all times, we praise thy name as we joyfully worship thee. We are grateful for all thy churches raising hymns of praise to thee and offering their tributes. Help us while thinking of thy resurrection upon the first day of the week to be thankful for our living Lord. We thank thee for the abiding truths of the Bible. May we live them and share them, we pray. Amen.

On Going to Church

Our church gives us the opportunity to worship God in union with other believers. We become aware of an enveloping sense of his presence. A true worship experience fills a deep need in our lives and brings a feeling of joy, because we have openly acknowledged God. The memory of this high spiritual hour draws us back to church, Sunday after Sunday. We think of God's goodness and of his majesty; we recognize his manifold blessings and pour out our adoration, our love, and our gratitude. We give ourselves anew to him and receive him anew in our hearts. We leave with our hearts inspired to live out his principle of love in the world, to be better representatives of his.

★　★　★

I was glad when they said to me,
   "Let us go to the house of the Lord!"
Our feet have been standing
   within your gates, O Jerusalem!

Jerusalem, built as a city
   which is bound firmly together,
to which the tribes go up,
   the tribes of the Lord,
as was decreed for Israel,
   to give thanks to the name of the Lord.
There thrones for judgment were set,
   the thrones of the house of David.

Pray for the peace of Jerusalem!
   "May they prosper who love you!
Peace be within your walls,
   and security within your towers!"

— *Ps. 122:1-7*

Begin, my tongue, some heav'nly theme,
And speak some boundless thing;
The mighty works or mightier name
Of our eternal King.

Tell of his wondrous faithfulness,
And sound his pow'r abroad;
Sing the sweet promise of his grace,
And the performing God.
— Isaac Watts, 1707 (1674-1748)

★　　★　　★

O Lord God of hosts, "the heavens are thine, and the earth also is thine; the world and all that is in it" (Ps. 89:11). Give us of thy steadfast love and faithfulness as we own thee as our Savior and Lord. May we express our love in offerings of gratitude and praise along with our material gifts. Amen.

The Word

Words are revealing; they transmit ideas. They lay bare the thoughts of the mind and disclose the nature of our being. By them, we judge one another. Jesus was called the Word. He was made flesh and came to the earth to disclose God to men. "In the beginning was the Word and the Word was God." He was full of truth and life. He helped to satisfy the longings of men's hearts to more fully understand the Creator. He was God with us, disclosing divine love in his manner of life and death. Our main task is to see God through him, to catch his spirit, to desire to please him.

★　★　★

And the Word became flesh and dwelt among us, full of grace and truth; we have beheld his glory, glory as of the only Son from the Father. — *John 1:14*

Beloved, let us love one another; for love is of God, and he who loves is born of God and knows God. He who does not love does not know God; for God is love. In this the love of God was made manifest among us, that God sent his only Son into the world, so that we might live through him. In this is love, not that we loved God but that he loved us and sent his Son to be the expiation for our sins. Beloved, if God so loved us, we also ought to love one another. No man has ever seen God; if we love one another, God abides in us and his love is perfected in us. — *1 John 4:7-12*

★　★　★

O Word of God Incarnate,
O Wisdom from on high,
O Truth unchanged, unchanging,
O Light of our dark sky:

We praise thee for the radiance
That from the hallowed page,
A lantern to our footsteps,
Shines on from age to age.
— W. W. How, 1867 (1823-1897)

★ ★ ★

O Lord, our God, how grateful we are for Jesus' coming to reveal thyself to us. We thank thee for the love and concern he demonstrated in his life for all men. May we know how powerful love is in the midst of hate and fear. May we love one another and so live that our lives proclaim the love that only thou canst give. Forgive our hateful, ugly ways. Amen.

Sharing

We cannot truly pray "Thy kingdom come" unless we are willing to share our Saviour. The gospel is true for all and it is our great joy to proclaim it. As his children we speak and act for him in the world by living the life of faith. We strive to see the rich, the poor, the educated, the uneducated as God sees them and love them as he loves them. God's grace releases man from self-pride and from deep distress and makes possible a noble and godly life. It is our joy to share the good news of the gospel.

★　★　★

I am the good shepherd; I know my own and my own know me, as the Father knows me and I know the Father; and I lay down my life for the sheep. And I have other sheep, that are not of this fold; I must bring them also, and they will heed my voice. So there shall be one flock, one shepherd. For this reason the Father loves me, because I lay down my life, that I may take it again. No one takes it from me, but I lay it down of my own accord. I have power to lay it down, and I have power to take it again; this charge I have received from my Father. — *John 10:14-18*

★　★　★

Give me a faithful heart,
Likeness to Thee,
That each departing day
Hence-forth may see
Some work of love begun
Some deed of kindness done,
Some wand'rer sought and won
Something for Thee.
　　　　　— Sylvanus D. Phelps,
　　　　　1816-1895

O God, strengthen us to live for thee at all times. Give us the courage to be faithful, brave, and true so others can see that our love for thee is real. Help us in grappling with the circumstances of life to find thy way to peace within. We thank thee for walking with us on our pilgrim journey through this world. May we take time to speak oft with thee. Amen.

Covetousness

To withhold our encouragement, our praise, and our prayers from our friends to whom they are due is a form of covetousness. It shows that we are envious of their fine accomplishments. This selfish spirit restricts life and takes away its joys. Strongly desiring and grasping the best for ourselves and our families does not give happiness. Love does not seek even what is its own, but a greedy person seeks more than his own. He is like the rich fool who built bigger and better barns for his wealth, which was all tangible. His life consisted solely of things; he had no inner riches of the soul.

★　★　★

. . . Take heed, and beware of all covetousness; for a man's life does not consist in the abundance of his possessions. — *Luke 12:15*

You shall not covet your neighbor's house; you shall not covet your neighbor's wife, or his manservant, or his maidservant, or his ox, or his ass, or anything that is your neighbor's. — *Ex. 20:17*

He who loves money will not be satisfied with money; nor he who loves wealth, with gain; this also is vanity. — *Eccles. 5:10*

Do not withhold good from those to whom it is due,
when it is in your power to do it.

— Prov. 3:27

★　★　★

O Jesus, Master, when today,
I meet, along the crowded way,
My burdened brothers — mine and thine —
May then through me thy Spirit shine.

Grant, too, that they my need may know,
As side by side we onward go —
An equal need of kindly thought,
And love like that which thou hast taught.

— Charles S. Newhall, 1842-1935

★ ★ ★

Deliver us, O God, from covetousness. May we be generous in words of praise and encouragement to those who merit them. Help us to walk in the ways of righteousness and in the paths of peace, we pray. Deliver us from the love of money, from trying to heap it up just for the sake of having it. Amen.

Wealth

Man can neither earn nor deserve God's gifts that are freely showered upon him. His belief causes him to accept the fact that God is the owner and giver of all things including his own life. These things are his temporarily and then some one else will enjoy them. What will he do with them? There are many possibilities when he realizes that he is debtor both to God and man. Unselfish uses will present themselves in connection with his church: worthy young people, old people, and perhaps many unique and individual needs that he alone can know and fulfill as he seeks to be faithful in his use of "coined personality."

. . . Man heaps up, and knows not who will gather! — *Ps. 39:6b*

> Better is a little with the fear of the Lord
> than great treasure and trouble with it.
> *— Prov. 15:16*

He who did not spare his own Son but gave him up for us all, will he not also give us all things with him? — *Rom. 8:32*

> He who has a bountiful eye will be blessed,
> for he shares his bread with the poor.
> *— Prov. 22:9*

And God is able to provide you with every blessing in abundance, so that you may always have enough of everything and may provide in abundance for every good work. — *2 Cor. 9:8*

> *May we thy bounties thus*
> *As stewards true receive,*
> *And gladly, as thou blessest us,*
> *To thee our first fruits give.*

And we believe thy word,
Though dim our faith may be;
Whate'er for thine we do, O Lord,
We do it unto thee.
— William W. How, 1823-1897

★　★　★

Our Father, we thank thee for thy generous gifts. May we use them with creative satisfaction in thy service. May we help in making some people more hopeful and life more worthwhile for them. May we have new experiences that will enrich life. May our love abound with knowledge. Bless all who sorrow and mourn; those who are sick and distressed, comfort. Bless thy ministers and the congregations that they serve. Grant that they may be true and faithful witnesses for thee. Amen.

On Growing

"I like the sowing and the reaping, but not the cultivating" was the remark of a workman as he planted a spring garden. Ah! the weeding, hoeing, feeding, and thinning of plants seem long and tedious tasks, but how necessary. While he sowed, he envisioned the abundant harvest but did not want to work for it. There can only be a garnering of good things in our lives by diligent effort and stern self-discipline. We can use time well in developing mentally, spiritually, and socially. We can aspire to become more acceptabe to God and man as we mature.

★ ★ ★

. . . No longer be children, tossed to and fro and carried about with every wind of doctrine, by the cunning of men. . . . Rather, speaking the truth in love, we are to grow up in every way into him who is the head, into Christ, from whom the whole body, joined and knit together by every joint with which it is supplied, when each part is working properly, makes bodily growth and upbuilds itself in love. — *Eph. 4:14-16*

> Sow for yourselves righteousness,
>   reap the fruit of steadfast love;
>   break up your fallow ground,
> for it is the time to seek the Lord,
>   that he may come and rain salvation upon you.
> — *Hos. 10:12*

★ ★ ★

> *To him that o'ercometh*
> *God giveth a crown,*
> *Thro' faith we shall conquer,*
> *Tho' often cast down;*

He, who is our Savior,
Our strength will renew,
Look ever to Jesus,
He'll carry you through.

— Horatio R. Palmer,
1834-1917

★　　★　　★

Dear God, we want to grow into stalwart Christians. We hate the sins that keep us stunted. We seek thy forgiveness and thy strengthening power in our lives. Help us to attain the spiritual aspirations of our souls. We need thee every hour to be our helper. Help us to strive manfully onward. Amen.

Within

What happens to us always happens from within. The family is hurt from within when husband and wife fail to communicate and fail in their vows of love. The church is hurt from within when the members fail to follow God's guidance. The nation is hurt from within by the disloyalty and treachery of a few citizens. On and on the failures go and where they stop is often tragic. What you do is important. You lend your strength or your weakness to that unit of society to which you belong. It is either helped or hindered by you. Are you a part of the world's problem or a part of the answer? Which am I?

★   ★   ★

Be gracious to me, O God, for men trample upon me;
    all day long foemen oppress me;
my enemies trample upon me all day long,
    for many fight against me proudly.
When I am afraid,
    I put my trust in thee:
In God, whose word I praise,
    In God I trust without a fear.
What can flesh do to me?

— *Ps. 56:1-4*

Behold, God is my salvation;
    I will trust, and will not be afraid.

— *Isa. 12:2*

★   ★   ★

I am trusting thee, Lord Jesus,
Trusting only thee;
Trusting thee for full salvation,
Great and free.

I am trusting thee for pardon;
At thy feet I bow;
For thy grace and tender mercy,
Trusting now.
> — Frances R. Havergal, 1874
> (1836-1879)

★　　★　　★

O God, we trust thee at all times but especially when things pile up around us so that we feel suffocated and cut off from normal living. May we add to the sum total of righteousness in the world by standing for justice and right. Help us not to add to the problems of home, church, or nation. May we put the "stubborn ounces" of our weight against wrong. We thank thee for giving us individually an opportunity to count for good. Amen.

Forgiving Love

His love covers a multitude of sin in our lives. Has your love ever covered a sin in the life of your fellowman? Forgiveness is the gift of God for all men. Who am I and who are you to condemn anyone when Christ has forgiven so much in us? Unless we forgive, we are excluding ourselves from this universal gift. He wants us to receive it and to extend it. He who forgives an offense exhibits God's love, but he who repeats a matter alienates a friend. How real is your love? How real is my love? Forgiveness expresses divine understanding. His love covered the transgressions of all his people.

★   ★   ★

Brethren, if a man is overtaken in any trespass, you who are spiritual should restore him in a spirit of gentleness. Look to yourself, lest you too be tempted. — *Gal. 6:1*

If you love those who love you, what credit is that to you? For even sinners love those who love them. And if you do good to those who do good to you, what credit is that to you? For even sinners do the same. And if you lend to those from whom you hope to receive, what credit is that to you? For even sinners lend to sinners, to receive as much again. — *Luke 6:32-34*

A new commandment I give to you, that you love one another; even as I have loved you, that you also love one another. By this all men will know that you are my disciples, if you have love one for another. — *John 13:34-35*

★   ★   ★

Lord, I would be thine alone,
Thee my only master own,
And, into thy likeness grown,
Live and love like thee;

By thy grace my heart renew,
Me with faith and pow'r endue,
Sanctify and make me new,
More and more like thee.

— Elisha A. Hoffman,
1839-1929

★　　★　　★

O God, we praise thee for thy mercy never ceasing. Purify our hearts and make us good. Help us to love our fellowman with such a pure, holy love that we will not have evil thoughts about him or repeat an ugly thing that may be real or only imagined. May we pass on thy forgiving grace to others. We thank thee for hearing our feeble prayers. Make us strong in thy strength, we pray. Amen.

God Is Spirit

What manner of life we can lead with God the Holy Spirit in us to guide and to comfort! The power of his Spirit is known in communion with God. Prayer is a discipline that keeps us in contact with Jesus Christ; it keeps the inner life under control; it causes us to love our neighbors; it increases and intensifies our desire to please God. It causes us to sense more vividly that God is Spirit and that he dwells in us. It causes us to accept his promise that our spirits will be triumphant. He demonstrated eternal life.

And do not fear those who kill the body but cannot kill the soul; rather fear him who can destroy both soul and body in hell. Are not two sparrows sold for a penny? And not one of them will fall to the ground without your Father's will. But even the hairs of your head are all numbered. Fear not, therefore; you are of more value than many sparrows. So every one who acknowledges me before men, I also will acknowledge before my Father who is in heaven; but who ever denies me before men, I also will deny before my Father who is in heaven. — *Matt. 10:28-33*

Spirit divine, attend our pray'r,
And make our heart thy home;
Descend with all thy gracious pow'r;
Come, Holy Spirit, come.

Come as the light! to us reveal
The truth we long to know;
Reveal the narrow path of right,
The way of duty show.

  — Andrew Reed, 1787-1862
    Adapted by Samuel Longfellow,
    1819-1892

Our Father in heaven, we thank thee for thy great concern. Thou hast said that our needs are known to thee before we speak and that they shall be supplied according to thy wisdom. How can we express our gratitude for thy goodness? Help us to give thee the honor due thy name by being constant in our worship and adoration. As we read thy word, open our eyes that we may behold wondrous things out of thy law. Be our companion and guide this day. Amen.

Intercessory Prayer

He taught the disciples to say, "Our Father who art in heaven," as they prayed. Intercessory prayer can be offered by a lone individual or by a group. Both types are necessary for spiritual development. It is our daily privilege and obligation to remember our friends and neighbors at the throne of grace. This is a spiritual activity that can be performed even on a sickbed while the body is recovering from an illness. All can participate in it with regularity. Fellowship through prayer is one of God's great gifts to men. It has great spiritual value.

★　★　★

Truly, truly, I say to you, he who believes in me will also do the works that I do; and greater works than these will he do, because I go to the Father. Whatever you ask in my name, I will do it, that the Father may be glorified in the Son; if you ask anything in my name, I will do it.

If you love me, you will keep my commandments. And I will pray the Father, and he will give you another Counselor, to be with you for ever, even the Spirit of truth, whom the world cannot receive, because it neither sees him nor knows him; you know him, for he dwells with you, and will be in you.

I will not leave you desolate; I will come to you. — *John 14:12-18*

★　★　★

O Master, let me walk with thee
In lowly paths of service free;
Tell me thy secret, help me bear
The strain of toil, the fret of care.

Teach me thy patience; still with thee
In closer, dearer company,
In work that keeps faith sweet and strong,
In trust that triumphs over wrong.
　　　　　— Washington Gladden, 1880
　　　　　(1836-1918)

May we, our Father, have thy peace in our hearts. Wilt thou be with those whose souls are sick and those whose bodies are sick. May we be patient with those who are slow to do and to learn. Be with all who have griefs to bear and those who are lonely and discouraged. Strengthen our faith in thee. Be with thy people scattered among the inhabitants of the earth. May their witness be a true and winsome one, we pray. Amen.

Our Father

A God whom our minds could grasp could not command our faith and our worship. God is "nearer than hands or feet" yet we fail to understand the distinctive privilege of being able to be in constant communion with him. Jesus came to reveal what God is like. He is like a Father. By his living, he imparted a richer quality to the concept of that word. In his youth when his parents found him in the temple, he asked, "Did you not know that I must be in my Father's house?" In his cry from the cross, he said, "Father, into thy hands I commit my spirit!"

And in praying do not heap up empty phrases as the Gentiles do; for they think that they will be heard for their many words. Do not be like them, for your Father knows what you need before you ask him. Pray then like this:

> Our Father who art in heaven,
> Hallowed be thy name.
> Thy kingdom come,
> Thy will be done,
> On earth as it is in heaven.
> Give us this day our daily bread;
> And forgive us our debts,
>   As we also have forgiven our debtors;
> And lead us not into temptation,
>   But deliver us from evil.
>
> — *Matt. 6:7-13*

Take the name of Jesus ever
As a shield from ev'ry snare;
If temptations round you gather,
Breathe that holy name in pray'r.

At the name of Jesus bowing,
Falling prostrate at his feet,
King of kings in heav'n we'll crown him,
When our journey is complete.

— Lydia Baxter, 1809-1874

★ ★ ★

Dear God and Father, we come to thee at this quiet hour because we adore thee and our hearts seek after thee — yea, they long for thee. We are grateful for all thy blessings. We thank thee for our lives that we may use in thy service. May their influence be for good. As we go about our daily tasks, keep our minds on thee. Help us not to stray from the path of right. Bless all with special needs this day. Amen.

Unafraid

Jesus was the only one at the crucifixion who was not afraid. The people composing the mob were afraid of the Roman rulers. The soldiers carrying out the orders were afraid of their superiors. Pilate was afraid of the Emperor. They all felt alone in their fear. Jesus was not afraid because he had surrendered to the Father's will. Jesus could say, "I am not alone, my Father is with me." We too can say, "I am not alone, my Father is with me." In the depths of our souls, God, the infinite, has set up a temple for his worship. From within, we have this source of courage. We need not fear what man can do.

★ ★ ★

For God did not give us a spirit of timidity but a spirit of power and love and self-control. . . . Take your share of suffering for the gospel in the power of God, who saved us and called us with a holy calling, not in virtue of our works but in virtue of his own purpose and the grace which he gave us in Christ Jesus ages ago . . . who abolished death and brought life and immortality to light through the gospel. . . . But I am not ashamed, for I know whom I have believed, and I am sure that he is able to guard until that Day what has been entrusted to me. — *2 Tim. 1:7-10, 12*

I will never fail you nor forsake you. — *Heb. 13:5b*

★ ★ ★

O for a faith that will not shrink,
Tho' pressed by every foe,
That will not tremble on the brink
Of any earthly woe!

That will not murmur or complain
Beneath the chast'ning rod,
But, in the hour of grief or pain,
Will lean upon its God.

— William H. Bathurst,
1796-1877

★ ★ ★

O God, we trust thee as did our fathers; they trusted and thou wast good to them. Keep us unafraid, because thou art within us ready to guide and direct our lives. Help us to live in such a manner that our faith may be revealed. If we cannot always understand the things that happen to us, we can trust thee. Amen.

Courage to Continue

It is easy to be pleasant when everything is going well, but it is difficult when things go wrong. What we really are shows then. The struggles of life make us noble or ignoble. Character develops slowly. God can make us persistent in the face of trials. Michelangelo took a marred piece of marble from the scrap heap and worked it into his famous statue of David. With God's help, we can work around our defects and turn them into assets. It is alone with him that we discover courage to continue. We become less concerned about ourselves and more concerned about others.

★ ★ ★

Not by might, nor by power, but by my Spirit, says the Lord of hosts. — *Zech. 4:6b*

As they were going along the road, a man said to him, "I will follow you wherever you go." And Jesus said to him, "Foxes have holes, and birds of the air have nests; but the Son of man has nowhere to lay his head." — *Luke 9:57-58*

And let us not grow weary in well-doing, for in due season we shall reap, if we do not lose heart. —*Gal. 6:9*

Therefore, my beloved brethren, be steadfast, immovable, always abounding in the work of the Lord, knowing that in the Lord your labor is not in vain. — *1 Cor. 15:58*

★ ★ ★

God is our strength and song,
And his salvation ours;
Then be his love in Christ proclaimed
With all our ransomed pow'rs.

Stand up, and bless the Lord;
The Lord your God adore;
Stand up, and bless his glorious name,
Henceforth forevermore.

— James Montgomery, 1771-1854

★　★　★

Our Father in heaven, hallowed be thy name. Forgive us for turning from thee and failing. Help us to depend upon thee and be persistent in following thee. Keep our feet upon the upward way even though our ascent is slow. We thank thee for being our ever-present help. We bless thy holy name and thank thee for the courage to continue. Amen.

Set Apart

I grew up thinking of the preacher as a special person, unique, set apart. This concept has grown to include all Christians. These set-apart ones are peculiar, not in their manner of dress nor in their pious sounding voices, but in their way of thinking and acting. The hours and days are to use in working out his plan. They think of every moment as sacred, usable in fulfilling their destiny. They are here to do God's will. Theirs is not the old-time one of testimony meetings. It is easy to talk but hard to do. They let their actions speak.

★　★　★

Lord, thou hast been our dwelling place
in all generations.
Before the mountains were brought forth,
or ever thou hadst formed the earth and the world,
from everlasting to everlasting thou art God.

Let the favor of the Lord our God be upon us,
and establish thou the work of our hands upon us,
yea, the work of our hands establish thou it.

— Ps. 90:1-2, 17

★　★　★

O Holy Savior, friend unseen,
Since on thine arm thou bidd'st me lean,
Help me thro'out life's changing scene,
By faith to cling to thee.

What tho' the world deceitful prove
And earthly friends and hopes remove;
With patient, uncomplaining love,
Still would I cling to thee.

— Charlotte Elliott, 1789-1871

O Holy Savior, help us to cling to thee throughout our lives as we fulfill our destiny in the world. Help us, our God, not to act in a peculiar manner, but to be conscious of our unique place in carrying out thy will. May we not be guilty of self-righteous attitudes. May we cooperate with thee in keeping our minds and our bodies free from distress and disease. Amen.

Grace

Grace is God's unmerited favor. It is a precious thing. It cost Jesus his life. Through it, we have free and unconditional forgiveness of sin. When a man leaves all and follows Christ, he can truly say that he has received grace. He is justified. It cost God much and it costs the recipient much, too. He must renounce his self-will and accept God's will. He cannot cling to anything but must leave all and follow him. It is learning to let Jesus be the Lord of life. Obey, believe. Believe, obey. Obedience makes faith real. This is the way out of bondage to ourselves. To live a life of obedience and discipleship is to follow the Way.

★   ★   ★

For by grace you have been saved through faith; and this is not your own doing, it is the gift of God — not because of works, lest any man should boast. For we are his workmanship, created in Christ Jesus for good works, which God prepared beforehand, that we should walk in them. — *Eph. 2:8-10*

Peace be to the brethren, and love with faith, from God the Father and the Lord Jesus Christ. Grace be with all who love our Lord Jesus Christ with love undying. — *Eph. 6:23-24*

. . . My grace is sufficient for you, for my power is made perfect in weakness. — *2 Cor. 12:9a*

★   ★   ★

Great Redeemer, we adore thee,
God of mercy, love, and grace;
Warm our hearts with thine own being,
May we see thy kindly face!

Great Redeemer, we adore thee,
God's great love to man thou art;
We adore thee, Great Redeemer,
Reign supreme in every heart.

— John Roy Harris, 1891-
Copyright 1940 by the
Sunday School Board of the
Southern Baptist Convention

★   ★   ★

Forgiving Father, we come out of our sin and bondage into thy-self. We cannot claim thy grace through our goodness, but we claim it through obedience to our Lord Jesus Christ. We thank thee that Jesus paid the price of our redemption, that through him our souls are saved. We thank thee for the gift of grace through Christ our Lord. Amen.

Our Classroom

Brother Lawrence's classroom was a kitchen. There he practiced the presence of God amid the menial tasks to which he had a great aversion. He surrendered himself completely to God and had faith as his rule of conduct. William Carey's school was a cobbler's shop where he placed before him a crude, handmade map of the world whose needs he envisioned. He became aware that his mission was to tell others the good news of the gospel. Our present environment is our place of learning. Our lessons may be difficult because we like to avoid testings, sufferings, and the humiliation of trials. We do not accept criticism and injustice graciously. These, however, are all opportunities to grow in grace unless we stand in our own way.

★　★　★

Humble yourselves therefore under the mighty hand of God, that in due time he may exalt you. Cast all your anxieties on him, for he cares about you. — *1 Pet. 5:6-7*

. . . He said to me, "My grace is sufficient for you, for my power is made perfect in weakness." I will all the more gladly boast of my weaknesses, that the power of Christ may rest upon me. For the sake of Christ, then, I am content with weaknesses, insults, hardships, persecutions, and calamities; for when I am weak, then I am strong. — *2 Cor. 12:9-10*

★　★　★

Lord, forever at thy side
Let my place and portion be:
Strip me of the robe of pride,
Clothe me with humility.

Meekly may my soul receive
All thy Spirit hath revealed;
Thou hast spoken; I believe,
Though the oracle be sealed.

— James Montgomery,
1771-1854

★   ★   ★

Our Father, deliver us from self-satisfaction and pride and fill us with thy humility. Free us from seeking glory for ourselves. Make our highest joy thy approval. Help us to do thy bidding. Make us to know that pride brings unhappiness to ourselves and others. May we be a blessing to our friends. May we be enabled to bear the hardships that are our lot as we strive to serve thee. Amen.

Peter, the Sinner

Many people have identified themselves with Peter, the weak sinner. God has used redeemed sinners throughout the Christian era to do his work. Someone has said, "Whom else could he use?" Men are his instruments in the world. When they have owned up to their offenses and accepted God's forgiveness, they have become available to do his work. They have depended on God to help them battle wrongdoing in themselves and in others. Like Peter, their failures have been ones of weakness, not treachery. Like Peter after his denial, they have been brought back into right relationship with God.

He destined us in love to be his sons through Jesus Christ, according to the purpose of his will, to the praise of his glorious grace which he freely bestowed on us in the Beloved. In him we have redemption through his blood, the forgiveness of our trespasses, according to the riches of his grace which he lavished upon us. For he has made known to us in all wisdom and insight the mystery of his will, according to his purpose which he set forth in Christ as a plan for the fullness of time, to unite all things in him, things in heaven, and things on earth. — *Eph. 1:5-10*

Holy Spirit, Truth Divine,
Dawn upon this soul of mine;
Breath of God, and inward Light,
Wake my spirit, clear my sight.

Holy Spirit, Love Divine,
Glow within this heart of mine;
Kindle every high desire;
Perish self in thy pure fire!

Holy Spirit, Power Divine,
Fill and nerve this will of mine;
By thee may I strongly live,
Bravely bear, and nobly strive.
— Samuel Longfellow, 1864

★   ★   ★

Dear God, give us open minds and receptive hearts willing to adjust when confronted with new ideas and truths. May we realize that thou art still revealing thyself to men as we are able to receive and respond to thy revelation. May we be instruments of thy will and purpose, willingly used of thee. Amen.

Peter, the Rock

Peter was unhappy over denying his master. In spite of all his weaknesses, Jesus could see and know that he had admirable qualities that should be developed. He was so overcome by Christ's forgiveness and great redeeming love that he became humble, not as a mark of shame but as an expression of joy in his master's service. His new-found humility made him teachable, because it was based on love and admiration of Christ's lowliness. By being willing to be nothing, he became Peter, the Rock. Can you identify with him?

★   ★   ★

He asked his disciples, "Who do men say the Son of man is?" And they said, "Some say John the Baptist, others say Elijah, and others Jeremiah or one of the prophets." He said to them, "But who do you say that I am?" Simon Peter replied, "You are the Christ, the Son of the living God." And Jesus answered him, "Blessed are you, Simon Bar-Jona! For flesh and blood has not revealed this to you, but my Father who is in heaven. And I tell you, you are Peter, and on this rock I will build my church, and the powers of death shall not prevail against it." — *Matt. 16:13b-18*

★   ★   ★

Glorious things of thee are spoken,
Zion, city of our God;
He, whose word cannot be broken,
Form'd thee for his own abode:
On the Rock of Ages founded,
What can shake thy sure repose?
With salvation's walls surrounded,
Thou may'st smile at all thy foes.

— John Newton, 1725-1807

Father, we thank thee that thy church was founded on the God-head of Christ as confessed by Peter. We thank thee for her sweet communion and solemn vows. Help us to love and pray for it and keep us loyal and true to it. Our Father, be near those who have not yet discovered the joys of worship within the community of believers. Be with us and guard our actions by which we proclaim what we believe. May we find God in our daily duties and be ever mindful of his presence within us as we perform them. Amen.

High Standards

High standards sometimes give one a sense of failure, but that does not mean that we need to lower them. Our dependence on God and his guidance may need to be much greater. Our periods of meditation and fellowship may need to be more regular and meaningful. Our thoughts and motives may need to be scrutinized more carefully. Our relationship to God may need to be more practical. We may need to take into account our finitude not as an excuse, but as a spur to a greater reliance on God's aid, by putting self aside and letting him have control. We can thus share in his ultimate victory.

★　★　★

Elijah was a man of like nature with ourselves and he prayed fervently that it might not rain, and for three years and six months it did not rain on the earth. Then he prayed again and the heaven gave rain, and the earth brought forth its fruit.

My brethren, if any one among you wanders from the truth and some one brings him back, let him know that whoever brings back a sinner from the error of his way will save his soul from death and will cover a multitude of sins. — *James 5:17-20*

Set your minds on things that are above, not on things that are on earth. — *Col. 3:2*

★　★　★

My soul, be on thy guard;
Ten thousand foes arise;
The hosts of sin are pressing hard
To draw thee from the skies.

O watch and fight and pray;
The battle ne'er give o'er;
Renew it boldly ev'ry day,
And help divine implore.

Ne'er think the vict'ry won,
Nor lay thine armor down;
Thy arduous work will not be done
Till thou obtain thy crown.
— George Heath, 1750-1822

★   ★   ★

O Father, we do implore thy help in our lives upon this earth and seek thy strength to battle against the wrongs we constantly encounter. Make us willing to answer the calls of duty that come to us along life's journey. May we serve thee with courage and faithfulness, in Jesus' name we pray. Amen.

Patience

Patience is an outgrowth of love. The more patient we are, the more like God we are becoming. Patience is hard "come by." Solving and adjusting many vexing and perplexing situations strengthens the self-control necessary for its development. When opinions conflict, there may be stormy periods while things are worked out. The discipline necessary for this accomplishment will help to make us vital. The new insights gained from such trials mature us and cause us to be more loving and lovable. The spirit of love wins over impatience and selfishness.

★ ★ ★

Count it all joy, my brethren, when you meet various trials, for you know that the testing of your faith produces steadfastness. And let steadfastness have its full effect, that you may be perfect and complete, lacking in nothing. If any of you lacks wisdom, let him ask God, who gives to all men generously and without reproaching, and it will be given him. — *James 1:2-5*

My son, do not despise the Lord's discipline
  or be weary of his reproof,
for the Lord reproves him whom he loves,
  as a father the son in whom he delights.
                    —*Prov. 3:11-12*

★ ★ ★

Come, gracious Lord, descend and dwell,
By faith and love, in ev'ry breast;
Then shall we know and taste and feel
The joys that cannot be expressed.

81

Come, fill our hearts with inward strength,
Make our enlarged souls possess,
And learn the height and breadth and length
Of thine eternal love and grace.

— Isaac Watts, 1709

★   ★   ★

O God, our present help, always ready to guide, we lift our voices to thee in praise and adoration. We thank thee for making it possible for us to develop in every part of our being. We thank thee that all of life is sacred. May our response to thee be always immediate and vivid as we grow in the life of faith and love. We thank thee for looking upon our hearts and understanding our intents. Amen.

Love Is a Catalyst

One aim of the church is to produce a new kind of person. God's love is the catalyst used to change man's whole scale of values and what a life he can lead. When love comes in contact with hate, it is dissolved and destroyed. When love faces hostility and persecution, life is still lived victoriously. Love makes a man spiritually aware. Love makes man hold fast in the most difficult time of testing. Love strengthens a man's spiritual fiber. Love makes us sure that God will bring to completion the good work he has begun in us.

★　★　★

And I am sure that he who began a good work in you will bring it to completion at the day of Jesus Christ. It is right for me to feel thus about you all, because I hold you in my heart, for you are all partakers with me of grace, both in my imprisonment and in the defense and confirmation of the gospel. For God is my witness, how I yearn for you all with the affection of Jesus Christ. And it is my prayer that your love may abound more and more, with knowledge and all discernment, so you may approve what is excellent, and may be pure and blameless for the day of Christ, filled with the fruits of righteousness which come through Jesus Christ, to the glory and praise of God. — *Phil. 1:6-11*

★　★　★

God is love; his mercy brightens
All the path in which we rove;
Bliss he wakes and woe he lightens:
God is wisdom, God is love.

Chance and change are busy ever;
Man decays and ages move;
But his mercy waneth never:
God is wisdom, God is love.
　　　　　　— Sir John Bowring, 1825
　　　　　　(1792-1872)

Our Father, we thank thee for a new and enriched life through Christ our Lord. May thy love abound more and more in our hearts until all hate, envy, or greed are dissolved and destroyed. Wilt thou broaden the scope of our knowledge. May we have the certainty that comes from doing thy will, so we can say as Paul did, "I am sure" of thee and of thy loving care and constant concern. Amen.

Do You Understand?

It is not given to finite man to understand the infinite God. We cannot fully understand Christianity and what it means. We know that God who made the world came to it and lived as man for a few short years and then passed through death to make eternal life available. He was the greatest man who ever lived. He was perfect; he was our divine God; he never sinned, therefore he had no desperate need for forgiveness himself. He prayed for those who wronged him and put him to death. It is only through our Christian experience when we submit to his influence and follow him that we begin to know who Jesus is. As life goes on and we continue to seek, he keeps on revealing himself to us.

Come to me, all who labor and are heavy laden, and I will give you rest. Take my yoke upon you, and learn from me; for I am gentle and lowly in heart, and you will find rest for your souls. For my yoke is easy, and my burden is light. — *Matt. 11:28-30*

He committed no sin; no guile was found in his lips. When he was reviled, he did not revile in return; when he suffered, he did not threaten; but he trusted to him who judges justly. He himself bore our sins in his body on the tree, that we might die to sin and live to righteousness. By his wounds you have been healed. For you were straying like sheep, but have now returned to the Shepherd and Guardian of your solus. — *I Peter 2:22-25*

Take my heart, O Father, take it;
Make and keep it all thine own;
Let thy Spirit melt and break it —
This proud heart of sin and stone.
— Anonymous, 1849

Our God and Father, we give thee thanks for Jesus who revealed thy love and grace to us. For his revelation of thy wisdom and truth, we give thee thanks. Open our eyes to the needs of those about us. Give us the wisdom that is "from above, peaceable, gentle and easy to be entreated, full of mercy and good fruits." Bestow thy mercy anew upon us and lead us in the way everlasting. Amen.

Positive and Hopeful

Great men see the positives in every situation. They are usually relaxed because they do what they can do best. Each of us is different, not better than others. Each of us has something to contribute. Each has his God-given ability as a means of self-expression and self-expansion. Each is responsible for using and developing his talent, accepting his own field of service with its limitations, eliminating tension.

. . . "Master, you delivered to me five talents; here I have made five talents more." His master said to him, "Well done, good and faithful servant; you have been faithful over a little, I will set you over much; enter into the joy of your master." And he also who had the two talents came forward saying, "Master, you delivered to me two talents; here I have made two talents more". . . . He also who had received the one talent came forward, saying, "Master I knew you to be a hard man, reaping where you did not sow, and gathering where you did not winnow; so I was afraid, and I went and hid your talent in the ground. Here you have what is yours." But his master answered him, "You wicked and slothful servant! . . . take the talent from him. . . ." — *Matt. 25:20-28*

Upon that painful road
By saints serenely trod,
Whereon their hallowing influence flowed,
Would we go forth, O God.

'Gainst doubt and shame and fear
In human hearts to strive,
That all may learn to love and bear,
To conquer self and live.

— Samuel Johnson, 1846

Our Father, may we be good and faithful servants of thine, making worthy use of our talents and abilities. May we learn to love each other as thou hast loved us. May we be easy to live with. May our spirits be generous and kind and hopeful. May we be happy in doing the things we can where we are. Amen.

Man's Source

God is the source of our existence. It follows logically that the purpose of it is to know him and to find in him the basis for living. In order to do this, we must become totally involved with him. We must not stop short of loving him with our whole being. He is the center of life. We must seek and find him for ourselves. Our experience of God is an individual one. This personal discovery goes on as continuously as birth and death. Studying the Bible will result in spiritual enrichment and cause us to stand in awe before our Lord.

★　　★　　★

Jesus then said . . . "If you continue in my word, you are truly my disciples, and you will know the truth, and the truth will make you free." — *John 8:31-32*

Do you not know that if you yield yourselves to any one as obedient slaves, you are slaves of the one whom you obey, either of sin, which leads to death, or of obedience, which leads to righteousness? — *Rom. 6:16*

Blessed are the pure in heart, for they shall see God. — *Matt. 5:8*

Seek the Lord and his strength,
seek his presence continuously!
　　　　　— Ps. 105:4

★　　★　　★

I need thee ev'ry hour,
Stay thou near by;
Temptations lose their pow'r
When thou art nigh.

I need thee ev'ry hour,
In joy or pain;
Come quickly and abide,
Or life is vain.

I need thee ev'ry hour,
Most Holy One;
O make me thine indeed,
Thou blessed Son.

— Annie S. Hawks,
1835-1918

★　　★　　★

Our Father, we need thee because thou art our source. Thou knowest our desires and aspirations. May they be worthy ones. May we have more purpose in prayer. Keep us confident and loyal in our love for thee and our fellowman. May we live out our faith this day and thus honor thee. Amen.

Are You Sure?

That question throws us into a dither because we are not sure. However, it does make us think. Are we sure that we are not paying too high a price for success? Is it the acknowledged or unacknowledged goal of our lives? If so, we may be unwittingly throwing life off center and endangering it by sacrificing dearly in order to attain this goal. Success could become an idol at whose demanding feet we are bowing down in adoration. Success can claim our whole being. God alone is worthy of our total involvement.

★ ★ ★

No one can serve two masters; for either he will hate the one and love the other; or he will be devoted to the one and despise the other. You cannot serve God and mammon.

Therefore I tell you, do not be anxious about your life; what you shall eat or what you shall drink, nor about your body, what you shall put on. Is not life more than food, and the body more than clothing?

Therefore do not be anxious, saying, "What shall we eat?" or "What shall we drink?" or "What shall we wear?" . . . but seek first his kingdom and his righteousness, and all these things shall be yours as well. — *Matt. 6:24-25, 31, 33*

★ ★ ★

I am resolved no longer to linger,
Charmed by the world's delight;
Things that are higher, things that are nobler,
These have allured my sight.

I am resolved to go to the Savior,
Leaving my sin and strife;
He is the true one, he is the just one,
He hath the words of life.

— Palmer Hartsough, 1844-1932

Our Father, help us not to be anxious about the material needs of life or what shall happen on the morrow, but anxious to live life at its best and fullest today, filling our places in the present. We thank thee for thy promise that if we seek thy kingdom first that we need not be anxious about the material things because thou art mindful of our needs. Amen.

Christ's Suffering

Christ, despised and rejected of men, was crucified for the world's unbearable burden of suffering. For him, this was a must in order to be Lord. For us, bearing rejection for Jesus' sake is a must in order to be true disciples. We must deny ourselves. We must wage a constant struggle against the flesh and the devil. We must take up our cross and follow him. We must let pride die and bear the shame of others' sins. We must forgive them and thus share their burden of guilt and in this way lighten their load. This is entering into the sufferings of Christ. The cross was rejection and shame.

★   ★   ★

Have this mind among yourselves, which you have in Christ Jesus, who, though he was in the form of God, did not count equality with God a thing to be grasped, but emptied himself, taking the form of a servant. . . . He humbled himself and became obedient unto death, even death on a cross. Therefore God has highly exalted him and bestowed on him the name which is above every name, that at the name of Jesus every knee should bow, in heaven and on earth, and under the earth, and every tongue confess that Jesus Christ is Lord, to the glory of God the Father.

—Phil. 2:5-11

★   ★   ★

Jesus, I my cross have taken,
All to leave, and follow thee;
Destitute, despised, forsaken,
Thou from hence my all shalt be;
Perish ev'ry fond ambition,
All I've sought or hoped or known;
Yet how rich is my condition:
God and heav'n are still my own!
— Henry F. Lyte, 1793-1847

93

Dear God, Savior of mankind, we praise and bless thy holy name. We thank thee for being our sinbearer. Strengthen us for the constant, daily struggle against evil in our lives. May we share the burdens of our friends and thus make them more bearable. May we be obedient followers. As we seek to serve thee, may we listen to thy guiding voice. Amen.

Attitudes

Our attitudes color our environment. In a sense they create it. Just as smog affects the air, so a sense of futility and defeat affects us by producing an adverse condition. Success is impossible when the subconscious mind wants to fail. God wants us to be happy in our unique place in the world. Its distinction may be that "no one can take your place." This is a complimentary remark, often heard by a person leaving one place to take up residence in another. It is true, but only in the sense that one had found "his place" and was filling it. "His place" moves with him to his new situation. He does not leave it behind to be filled.

God is our refuge and strength,
a very present help in trouble.
Therefore we will not fear though the
earth should change,
though the mountains shake in the
heart of the sea;
though its waters roar and foam,
though the mountains tremble with
its tumult. . . .
"Be still, and know that I am God.
I am exalted among the nations,
I am exalted in the earth!"
— *Ps. 46:1-3, 10*

O Joy that seekest me through pain,
I cannot close my heart to thee;
My heart restores its borrowed ray,
That in thy sunshine's glow its day
May brighter, fairer be.

95

O Cross that liftest up my head,
I dare not ask to hide from thee,
I lay in dust life's glory dead,
And from the ground there blossoms red
Life that shall endless be.

— George Matheson, 1842-1906

★   ★   ★

Our Father, we give thee back the life that thou didst bestow. We give it back to thee in love and in service and in gratitude for thy salvation. We thank thee that thou art love and for thy willingness to share thyself with people. Teach us to learn and obey thy lessons. Teach us to honor thee and to be prompt in serving thee. Forgive us and help us to be forgiving. Amen.

Staid

The word "staid" carries with it the idea of fixed, settled. When we pray, "Keep our hearts and minds staid on thee," we are asking God to make us stable, unwavering followers. It is good to have a fixed point in life, a point from which there is no bending. Christ is the Christian's compass to keep him going in the right direction. He does not want us to be tossed about with every wind of doctrine or with the whims of others. He wants us to have the compass-like quality of pointing the way.

★　★　★

If any of you lacks wisdom, let him ask God, who gives to all men generously and without reproaching, and it will be given him. But let him ask in faith, with no doubting, for he who doubts is like a wave of the sea that is driven and tossed by the wind. For that person must not suppose that a double-minded man, unstable in all his ways, will receive anything from the Lord. — *James 1:5-8*

> I keep the Lord always before me;
> because he is at my right hand, I shall
> not be moved.
>
> *— Ps. 16:8*

★　★　★

Amazing grace! how sweet the sound,
That saved a wretch like me!
I once was lost, but now am found,
Was blind, but now I see.

'Twas grace that taught my heart to fear,
And grace my fears relieved;
How precious did that grace appear
The hour I first believed!
— John Newton, 1725-1807

Our Father, we thank thee for a fixed point in life, so we cannot lose our way. Keep our hearts and minds staid on thee, we earnestly pray. We thank thee for thy transforming power in all the experiences of life. Keep us loyal, courageous and strong in our stand for thee. May our lives point in the right direction. This we pray for all thy followers in Jesus' name. Amen.

Catch His Spirit

The Christians' invisible assets are love, spiritual strength, and concern for others. The most important thing they can do is — catch the spirit of Jesus Christ. This spirit of love is God's great gift. It saves mankind and causes him to be unselfish in his love for others. They are to express this attitude not only toward the Christian community, but toward the world where they are being tested and tried. Our love toward people makes it easier for them to discover Christ for themselves. A man with a vital faith lives it out in daily life. Christ is his companion and his spiritual power has an extraordinary effect on others.

Do not plan evil against your neighbor
who dwells trustingly beside you.
Do not contend with a man for no reason
when he has done you no harm.
— *Prov. 3:29-30*

My son, keep my words
and treasure up my commandments with you;
keep my commandments and live,
keep my teachings as the apple of your eye;
bind them on your fingers,
write them on the tablet of your heart.
— *Prov. 7:1-3*

Good sense makes a man slow to anger,
and it is his glory to overlook an offense.
— *Prov. 19:11*

★   ★   ★

Would you live for Jesus, and be always pure and good?
Would you walk with him within the narrow road?
Would you have him bear your burden, carry all your load?
Let him have his way with thee.

Would you have him make you free, and follow at his call?
Would you know the peace that comes by giving all?
Would you have him save you so that you can never fall?
Let him have his way with thee.

— Cyrus S. Nusbaum, 1861-1937

★   ★   ★

O Lord, our eternal God, help us always to have the right attitude toward life and the manner in which we live it. Give us a sense of true responsibility for our influence upon others. May the potentialities for good in us develop in order to bring happiness to our homes and friends. May we truly love all people. Amen.

Wonder

Little children are pleased with everything because they have a sense of astonishment, of awe. The feel of green grass under bare feet in the spring, the color and form of the tiniest flower by the wayside, the blue sky with white clouds overhead, the sunset, hills and valleys, rivers and oceans are a transport of delight to them. They lose themselves completely and are supremely happy with the earth's bountiful beauty. As they grow into adulthood, they often lose the art of complete self-forgetfulness and life becomes less awesome and many times burdensome. What a pity for man ever to be bored amid the splendid surroundings of nature.

★   ★   ★

The earth is the Lord's and the fulness thereof,
the world and those who dwell therein;
for he has founded it upon the seas,
  and established it upon the rivers.
Who shall ascend the hill of the Lord?
  And who shall stand in his holy place?
He who has clean hands and a pure heart,
  who does not lift up his soul to what is false,
  and does not swear deceitfully.
He will receive blessing from the Lord,
  and vindication from the God of his salvation.

— Ps. 24:1-5

★   ★   ★

All things bright and beautiful,
All things great and small,
All things wise and wonderful;
Our Father made them all.

101

Cold wind in the winter,
Pleasant summer sun,
Ripe fruits in the garden;
He made them ev'ry one.

— Cecil F. Alexander, 1848
(1818-1895)

* * *

Our Father, we thank thee for eyes to see the beauty of the earth, for lips to tell of thy goodness. We thank thee for the birds with their sweet songs and lovely feathers; for the bright flowers with their messages of hope and love; for the beauty of childhood; for the aspirations of youth; and for the maturity of adulthood. May we have a childlike reverence in our hearts for them. Amen.

Our Guide

Marcus Aurelius said, "The greatest part of what we say and do being unnecessary, if a man takes this away, he will have more leisure and less uneasiness." The Bible would guide us into pleasant paths if we would let it. It tells us to judge not. Why? Only God knows the truth of a situation and only he can judge justly. It tells us not to take up a reproach against our neighbor. Why? We are to love our neighbors as ourselves. It tells us to be faithful. Why? This makes us pliable for God's use. He can make us what we ought to be. It tells us not to let the sun go down on our wrath. Why? Fresh hurts are more easily healed than neglected gangrenous ones.

★　★　★

I will sing to the Lord as long as I live;
　I will sing praise to my God while I have being.
May my meditation be pleasing to him,
　for I rejoice in the Lord.

— Ps. 104:33-34

Let the words of my mouth and the meditation of my heart
　be acceptable in thy sight,
O Lord, my rock and my redeemer.

— Ps. 19:14

I will meditate on thy precepts,
　and fix my eyes on thy ways.
— Ps. 119:15

★　★　★

Father in Heaven, who lovest all,
O help thy children when they call,
That they may build from age to age
An undefiled heritage.

Teach us delight in simple things,
And mirth that has no bitter springs;
Forgiveness free of evil done,
And love to all men 'neath the sun.

— Rudyard Kipling, 1865-1936

★   ★   ★

O God, our guide and counsellor, may we live this day in serene, firm kindness as we disregard things and value persons. May we know the value of forgetting ourselves and loving others so that our influence may be powerful for good. We thank thee that for every cross thou dost give the strength to bear it. May we be noble in the loftiest sense of the word. May we esteem and love all people. May we be normal, uncomplicated persons. Amen.

Be Considerate

Punctual people are usually trustworthy. They are considerate. They respect your time and your interests. If something happens to keep them from being prompt at a scheduled hour, they let it be known as soon as possible. Habitual tardiness indicates selfishness and unconcern for other people. To enter a church service late is disrupting to the congregation as well as the minister. To enter a concert late is uncomplimentary to the artists as well as to the audience. Be punctual and thereby express thoughtfulness. Consideration for others is a Christian virtue.

And as you wish that men would do to you, do so to them.
— Luke 6:31

For everything there is a season, and a time for every matter under heaven. *— Eccles. 3:1*

"He who is faithful in a very little is faithful also in much; and he who is dishonest in a very little is dishonest also in much."
— Luke 16:10

He whose ear heeds wholesome admonition will abide among the wise. He who ignores instruction depises himself, but he who heeds admonition gains understanding. The fear of the Lord is instruction in wisdom, and humility goes before honor.
— Prov. 15:31-33

None of us lives to himself, and none of us dies to himself.
— Rom. 14:7

★   ★   ★

Why do you wait, dear brother,
Oh, why do you tarry so long?
Your Savior is waiting to give you
A place in his sanctified throng.

105

What do you hope, dear brother,
To gain by a further delay?
There's no one to save you but Jesus,
There's no other way but his way.
— George F. Root, 1820-1895

★   ★   ★

Our Father, we would not be tardy in thanking thee for thy many gracious gifts. May we not be tardy in performing our obligations at home, at school, or at church. Help us to be mindful of all the people that our lives touch. Help us understand how they feel about things and to ponder their perspective. May we not be slack in our work and in the keeping of our appointments. Amen.

Adaptability

Learning to work with circumstances does not mean conforming. It does not indicate weakness, but the opposite — strength. It shows understanding and a willingness to yield. It shows a lack of self-centeredness which is stubborn and obstinate. In other words, it is finding and working out a religious outlook on life. The nearer we are to Christ, the nearer we are to each other and the more readily we can work out an understanding in difficult situations. There will always be some conflicting opinions as we live day by day surrounded by human beings.

★ ★ ★

Not that I complain of want; for I have learned, in whatsoever state I am, to be content. I know how to be abased, and I know how to abound; in any and all circumstances I have learned the secret of facing plenty and hunger, abundance and want. I can do all things in him who strengthens me.

Yet it was kind of you to share my trouble. And you Philippians yourselves know that in the beginning of the gospel, when I left Macedonia, no church entered into partnership with me in giving and receiving except you only. — *Phil. 4:11-15*

★ ★ ★

Faithful, O Lord, thy mercies are,
A rock that cannot move;
A thousand promises declare
Thy constancy of love.

Thou waitest to be gracious still;
Thou dost with sinners bear;
That, saved, we may thy goodness feel,
And all thy grace declare.

Its streams the whole creation reach,
So plenteous is the store;
Enough for all, enough for each,
Enough for evermore.

— Charles Wesley, 1707-1788

★   ★   ★

Holy Father, help us stand for right in a cool-headed, courageous and unselfish manner in circumstances that may be safe or unsafe. Help us to realize that wherever we are or whatever the surroundings, thou art with us. Nothing can separate us from thee. Give us courage to be unafraid of life and to live with contentment. Amen.

Scraps of Time

Bits of time left over between tasks are valuable and can be used to accomplish many things. The person who plans ahead can have a small book in his or her pocket or handbag. When unexpected moments of waiting arise, the mind can be employed with worthwhile thoughts rather than with irritable ones. Some people use these short interludes in silent meditation and prayer. There are daily tasks that do not require concentration and the time they consume can be used in praise to God. Time is too precious to lose.

★ ★ ★

So teach us to number our days
that we may get a heart of wisdom.
— *Ps. 90:12*

"Lord, let me know my end,
and what is the measure of my days;
let me know how fleeting my life is!
Behold, thou hast made my days a few handbreadths,
and my lifetime is as nothing in thy sight.
Surely every man stands as a mere breath!"
— *Ps. 39:4-5*

. . . They asked him, "Lord, will you at this time restore the kingdom to Israel?" He said to them, "It is not for you to know times or seasons which the Father has fixed by his own authority. But you shall receive power when the Holy Spirit has come upon you; and you shall be my witnesses in Jerusalem and in all Judea and Samaria and to the end of the earth." — *Acts 1:6-8*

★ ★ ★

All for Jesus! all for Jesus!
All my beings's ransomed powers:
All my tho'ts and words and doings,
All my days and all my hours.
— Mary D. James

Eternal God, as we consider our days and how fleeting they are, help us to adjust to new ways, for change and growth are twins. We thank thee for the experience of having been led by thee. As we look back over our lives, we can detect thy guiding hand. For this, we are truly grateful. We praise thee and bless thy name and seek thy nearness all the way. Amen.

Happiness

Robert Ingersoll said, "The time to be happy is now, the place to be happy is here, the way to be happy is to make others so." We could create a more pleasant situation with others through co-operation rather than competition. We cannot be happy by making ourselves or our careers the center of the universe. Happiness involves the interest and welfare of others, above our own. It comes as the result of mature thinking and living, of adult attitudes. In competing, there is constant comparison one with another and a desire to be superior. Great men are humble and kind. They compete with their own records rather than that of others. Happiness is habit-forming.

★ ★ ★

Bless the Lord, O my soul;
    and all that is within me, bless his holy name!
Bless the Lord, O my soul,
    and forget not all his benefits,
who forgives all your iniquity,
    who heals all your diseases,
who redeems your life from the Pit,
    who crowns you with steadfast love and mercy,
who satisfies you with good as long as you live
    so that your youth is renewed like the eagle's.
— Ps. 103:1-5

★ ★ ★

Immortal Love, forever full,
Forever flowing free,
Forever shared, forever whole,
A never-ebbing sea!

The healing of his seamless dress
Is by our beds of pain;
We touch him in life's throng and press,
And we are whole again.

O Lord and Master of us all,
Whate'er our name or sign,
We own thy sway, we hear thy call,
We test our lives by thine.

— John G. Whittier, 1807-1892

★　　★　　★

O heavenly Father, we thank thee for thy forgiving love and mercy, for thy healing power in sickness and for thy redeeming grace. Wilt thou take away the strain and stress of our lives and fill them with thy peace. Help us to love our fellow-man sincerely. May we grow in the likeness of Jesus. Amen.

Minutes and Money

Minutes and money are valuable according to our use of them. Either can be misused or dissipated. They are both essential elements of life as we live it. We think of minutes as God's gift, but often fail to realize that money is his gift, too. God gives the power and the ability to accumulate wealth. All things are his and he gives them to us temporarily. Many people think they would be generous if, after giving, there was much to spare. The only way we can prove our liberality is by giving all we can out of our present possessions. If we cannot supply a great need or endow a college, that does not excuse us from supplying a lesser need nearby.

★　★　★

"Behold, to the Lord your God belong heaven and the heaven of heavens, the earth with all that is in it." — *Deut. 10:14*

> The earth is the Lord's and the fulness thereof,
>   the world and those who dwell therein;
> for he has founded it upon the seas,
>   and established it upon the rivers.
>
> — *Ps. 24:1-2*

> "For every beast of the forest is mine,
>   the cattle on a thousand hills.
> I know all the birds of the air,
>   and all that moves in the field is mine."
>
> — *Ps. 50:10-11*

"The silver is mine, and the gold is mine, says the Lord of hosts." — *Hag. 2:8*

★　★　★

> *All things are thine; no gift have we,*
> *Lord of all gifts, to offer thee,*
> *And hence, with grateful hearts today,*
> *Thy own before thy feet we lay.*

Thy will was in the builder's thought;
Thy hand unseen amidst us wrought;
Thro' mortal motive, scheme, and plan,
Thy wise eternal purpose ran.

— John G. Whittier, 1807-1892

★　★　★

Our God and Lord, we praise thy holy name and hallow it. May thy kingdom come and thy will be done. May we of thy bounteous trust to us bring an offering to thee. Keep us from the love of money and give us faithful hearts. We wish to consecrate our talents, time, and love to thee along with our material gifts. Amen.

Christian People

People are the instruments of God. He carries out his purposes and does his work through them. He sent Jesus as a person to teach men. This he did mostly by his actions; that love is never-failing; that men ought always to pray; that he is our friend, and that he is forgiving. He also taught that God expects us to trust him, to serve him, and to love him with our whole being. He desires that we should be sensitive to his Spirit through whom he continues to reveal himself and through whom he guides us.

★ ★ ★

"Father, I desire that they also, whom thou hast given me, may be with me where I am, to behold my glory which thou hast given me in thy love for me before the foundation of the world. O righteous Father, the world has not known thee, but I have known thee; and these know that thou hast sent me. I made known to them thy name, and I will make it known, that the love with which thou hast loved me may be in them, and I in them."

—John 17:24-26

He was praying in a certain place, and when he ceased, one of his disciples said to him, "Lord, teach us to pray, as John taught his disciples." *— Luke 11:1*

★ ★ ★

More like Jesus would I be,
Let my Savior dwell in me;
Fill my soul with peace and love,
Make me gentle as a dove;
More like Jesus, while I go.
Pilgrim in this world below;
Poor in spirit would I be;
Let my Savior dwell in me.

—Fanny J. Crosby, 1820-1915

Dear Savior, how grateful we are for thy coming to earth to speak with men. We thank thee for teaching us how to live the abundant life. Take away our sinful thoughts and make us pure within. Help us to be more like thee when we pray, more like thee day by day. Help us to discern thy will through the leading of thy Holy Spirit. We thank thee for him. Amen.